Random expat thoughts

Ana Maria Gonzalez de la Rosa

BookLeaf Publishing

Presentation by *BookLeaf Publishing*

Web: www.bookleafpub.com

E-mail: info@bookleafpub.com

ISBN : 9789357210393

First edition 2022

DEDICATION

To my husband and children.

TO BE BRAVE

Some people call it destiny,
they don't believe it can be mold
but who comes to dare is happy,
tries and always achieves more.

You wake up in a new site
everything looks alien to you,
Where have you arrived now?
Nothing has been random, for sure.

You open your eyes and the curtains,
and want to create a brand new routine,
you go out to the world and feel immortal,
with this worthy of admiration mettle.

You left behind your old life
friends, buddies and neighbors,
your home, food and family
your job and fixed salary.

And you know that this adventure is
the best one in all your life
even though it can be tough
and you fall on your knees and doubt.

Suddenly some fear ambushes,
you think is better to go back
to there, where will wait always
your people, your home, your town…

When time passes by you discover that
that is not true. No one is waiting for you.
And maybe is that now you are
something better than you used to.

And yes, it breaks you inside.
And you may frequently cry,
But you know that change is good,
and crying has cleared your mood.

You rise and keep on,
now stronger
shaking the dust,
You laugh from your luck!

Being brave will never be
a reason to regret for.
Let's leave that for those
who dies with their dreams off.

MIGRANT

I have a baggage stuffed with dreams
I finished it last night while everybody slept.
I put in it my challenges, secrets and strength,
which I will take hence everywhere.

There, where I go, if there's a return I don't
know.
Will I regret my own choice?
I might not find friends as I have them now,
but is not a friend seeking for what I go for.

What to search then, from my homeland away?
to live fearless? a second language to learn?
Where I was born and grew up,
children can't play safely outside anymore.

Diverse obstacles are here and there,
life has taught me to walk on the way,
triumphant getting rid any difficulty,
giving up is not something we do in my country.

We have courage, wit, illusions and faith,
we are sincere, resilient and valiant,
we put the soul in games and songs
that have been our heritage for all life long.

We know the real happiness recipe
but is not only our, we want to share it
with anyone who ask for and treasure it
because sharing is part of our identity.

Now that I leave my beloved country
I find an eclectic, fascinating site.
I don't believe that a land in the Mundi
could be considered the greatest of all.

We all habit this beautiful world
and will cry and laugh, be down and up.
A place to live, some people will find,
a place to die, not anyone can.

So I go, unlimited, chasing chimeras,
with firm steps, no filters nor masks.
Enchanted, I accept this new phase.
The day is here! The wait is over!

Don't ask if I intend to be back,
but nostalgically remind of me
as I will think of you in the dawn
every single and constant day.

I go now, because we all know
whos many times say goodbye
doesn't really want to, but…

I ardently yearn this journey to start.

THE GOOD CHANGE

I dusted off the forces that I kept yesterday
in the closet of comfort and routine.
I looked for an outfit that would magically fit
with my roots and my day by day wings.

What I found has not stopped amazing me.
Is so big the world and yet so small,
I look at my side and find blue and green,
views I wish I have when I get old.

An ahuehuete, a cedar and a tall oak,
a bamboo, eucalyptus and a jacaranda.
A gannet always reminds me of Diego,
and the night is all a Tamayo canvas.

By downtown I walked for a moment,
found nice frontages, alive colors,
street sellers, an old broken lantern
and a musician playing old time notes.

Birds in my town go to sleep by six p.m.
Here they keep partying up to ten.
My land is known for suffer the drought,
here I got an umbrella, rain hasn't stopped.

I feel like home, I feel strong,
as if I had a brand new soul.
I have met again with that part of mine
which for a long time I forgot that I had.

All here is the same but different though.
Sometimes, in the middle of the crowd
I try to be nice and look in the eyes…
In spite of my effort, not always I can.

I discovered, bytheway, it is not just me,
there are many countrymen I can see here.
Getting over their fears for don't let
finish the day with anything met.

I will not let down my people, my land.
I will always its name put in high, so high,
where only the valiant eagle can reach,
and the coldest wind's song can be heard.

This trust that today fills my soul
with any who asks, I would like to share
with those interested in calmly know
these thoughts that now burstly come.

If you fear the change or a new path
You may keep your stable life
but if for a new story you decide,
don't let yourself stop by anyone.

The hardest part of living a dream
is to decide and the first step give.
When suddenly a warm hug you need,
without realizing, will have past a year.

You will see the sky, thinking in silence
that all have been good, nothing in vain.
You will feel that hidden cheer that borns
when you got the strength from where? who
knows.

And will see, at the end, the world is the same.
Sun brightens equally here or there.
But something inside you changed for good,
and you know for sure, you would do it again.

TO MY CHILDREN

I don’t ask you to understand
the decisions we take now.
Time will come for you to have
your own steps to guide.

I want you to learn to be strong,
to with no trying not to give up
and if possible, better yet,
don’t give up after trying even.

To always wear a smile
wherever the place you were,
to learn with no hurries to ride,
and enjoy being outside.

That you know the world is more
than just an empty shopping mall,
that you can get too far
if for the effort you decide.

That you can make friends
in any part of the world,
no matter if your ways
come from different roads.

That all of us are different
but all of us have a soul
and we must always be traten
with respect and with calm.

That is better to be prepared
and be ready for anything,
that is not worthy believe
that you just know a little.

That time passes quickly
and in less than a blink
not on purpose we have on
our not accomplished dreams.

But the most important thing
I want your mind to keep
is that even if we were apart,
forever you will be in my heart.

Carry always with you
the values we have taught
they are, I tell you for sure,
the treasure you need the most.

Do love much your siblings,
never stop helping them,
dad and mom love you, kids
and know you will take good care.

The adventures we have lived
sometimes have been hard,
but you always made us feel
strong to carry them out.

We are always proud
of having you as our children.
Your older days will come
and with them your own riddles.

Forgive if we have failed,
we just look for you the best,
but you will know someday
how tangled is to find a place.

And if perhaps you don't find it
you will have to create your own.
Let it be a place where you feel
you make a better world.

Always forward and loving,
strong, fearless and smiling,
don't let any command
to take your happiness down.

Always look in the eye,
never regret give a hand,

that any effort we make
let it not be in vain.

I don’t ask you to understand
the intention of your parents.
Time will come for you to have
to sail your own seas farest.

MY LONELINESS

You hadn't visited me long time ago
I had forgotten the time we had before,
when sky was more sad and nothing cheered me
up,
I lost some friends or lost an old love.

And now you come to share time with me again,
Suddenly I find you disturbing my days
But is different. I feel you close and I smile,
maybe the age has made me change that.

You are my accomplice in these times.
You silently laugh when I tell you my plans,
as if you knew that I'm not capable of anything,
but I don't mind you, I just keep inventing.

Every morning you come and a coffee invite
and me, defenseless, accept and lose my time.
By night with a wine and surrendered by stars,
I tell you my dreams which you pretend to like.

Only with you, my biggest contrasts I unveil.
Sometimes, I believe anything I can achieve,
some other, that I'm a mess and I will fail.

You encourage me to try and then fill me with fear.

Solitude: you inspire me, fear me, kill me,
In you I find me, lose me, fall down and get up.
Because only with you I really meet myself,
I can hear the music I love to play.
This is an emotional cocktail, amazingly prepared,
Comes with charm, with bitterness and pain.
It's a scream, a cute story and a rude game,
and my best push to start all over again.

I don't want any company today, I love my freedom.
To fill my mind with riddles and clear them,
to create secrets to keep with me and no one else.
My favorite and yet most hated place… my loneliness.

DEPRESSION, MY FRIEND

You assault me again
and I used to say
you were an invention
and you weren't real.

That who feel you
is because they want to
that is easy to beat you
they just need to wish to.

But you got me, dear…
I had a cloudy day,
I felt without air
and couldn't think clear.

My mood was low
all day face downward
and a voice told:
"Look at you, coward!"

I don't want to hear you!
This is a good thing!
I can get used to
carry everything.

I don’t want to eat.
don’t rest while sleep,
how is possible this,
you affecting me?

It is so surprising
your power in me,
some days I can feel
you came here to kill.

I can do nothing
to feel better a bit,
is best to give up
and just disappear…

Depression, my friend,
come hug me today.
I want you to know
that life can be great.

That there’s a world there
fulfilled with beauty
and getting fresh air
cleans the sooty.

Or at least takes you away
from me for a while,
and you leave me lay

a shooting smile.

That time I avail
and I feel again
as I can achieve
something being me.

And this time, stronger,
I will fearless yell
I beat you, stranger!
and it feels so well.

TO MY MOTHER

You thought you wouldn't cry
when the time finally came
for us say goodbye
when I had to take my plane.

As it was expected,
we couldn't hold
and we cried like it does
any little girl or boy.

I left and you stayed
but you're here with me
because whatever happens
I find you in the swing.

You suppose I don't think about you
If I don't call or I don't write to you.
It's not like that, don't you believe,
I always carry you with me.

There is your face in the morning
when I pour a coffee to myself,
in the photo than in the window
I placed when I got here.

There is your scent in the closet
when i look for the old coat
that you gave me as a present
and I always bring it on.

There is your caress on my face
when i walk in the morning
and some wind with its breath
sweet and soft accompanies me.

There iss your advice in my ear
whenever I don't know what to do,
I think how would it be with you?
What would be your procedure?

So, there you stayed
but you live here with me,
don't you know that like art,
You fill my path with peace?

I carry your blood, your genes,
your lessons and blessings.
I say this so you remember:
In my heart you always live.

EXPAT WIFE

Oh woman in love!
I know how you feel today.
You left your past life
and you did it for love.

You never imagined
moving to other country
but it appeared your beloved
and you said "yes" quickly.

"Yes", but you didn't know
all that it implied
"Yes" to be day by day
the one who silent remains.

"Yes" to the formalities,
to travel maybe alone,
to look for a new home,
to change your life entirely.

"Yes" to learn a new language,
"yes" to a brand new culture,
you accepted the full package
of having a crazy future.

And suddenly you understood
that this is not temporary,
that to your old home you could
not come back in a century.

And suddenly your title,
your profession is useless,
you feel inside a circle,
with no escape from it, hopeless.

You never had been
before at home so long,
doing laundry and cleaning,
don't get what's going on?

Your old group of friends
don't respond to your messages,
those nights out were nonsense,
they don't even like your images.

Some doubts perhaps appear
and you might want to go back,
but is love the only thing
that helps you keep the path.

Remember: This is your story,
no one is living for you.
Create great memories

while you remain with this view.

Make up if you want to,
keep your head always up,
let them all believe you are strong,
at the end, that is the only truth.

Take care of mind and body,
don't let your sunset be sad,
and never keep as a secret
the gifts provided by God.

Yo are much better person
than you believe you are now,
it is brave and worth
who changes life for love.

Expat lady, be afraid no more,
for sure one day you will
see all this toil's reward,
for your tireless love indeed.

And if someday you fall,
fall over completely.
Don't ever quit along
if you don't plan to forget it.

NOWADAYS

Some days I wake up with my dreams slept
fixed my hair but quiet my yell,
my obstinate neurons exploring a riddle
from which, they will give up in the middle.

I explode in questions, how? why? when? for
what?
How is that we sighted to this cardinal point?
when we lost faith? why we lost course?
why to keep trying if everything is wrong?

I ask myself, is that fragil the human race,
that need to end with its brother in order to feel
peace?
So much genius and time invested in vain,
So much wit destroyed by mundane treats.

I see ambition without effort and madness
without passion,
proud without achievements, mentors with no
inspiration.
Frustrated wishes, histories that will no longer
be,

shadows that loudly asks for a owner to
accompany.

Everybody easily connect to the cloud,
and forget to plug in the soul to what matters,
to people, to the freshness of an ardent sight,
to the soft breath that is daily supported.

Suddenly some detail restores the hope…
A couple of elderly walking hand by hand,
a child who stops by just for a flower,
A straight judge punishing the inhuman.

Sporters compete without humiliate their rivals,
scientists discover new remedies to illness,
musicians compose new partitures
which make us forget of all our evils.

Some nights I sleep with the dreams awake,
the hair made a mess but in order my mind,
with the warm peace of whom believed was
dead
the future and sudden, a lucky charm finds.

As a fountain in the park, as a children
playground,
of ups and downs the liferoad is filled out.
Joys and misfortunes rise us and turn down,

but always load our journey with a purpose to survive.

TIME ROLLING

Time doesn't pass in vain
I know because I see in my hands
the marks of many handshakes
from the weariness every day.

I know it because all change
and nothing changes at the same time.
No matter how much we look for calm,
there is no thing that remains intact.

Changes your voice and your gaze,
that smile that used to rise
with every moment insane,
sometimes tries to hide.

It stays your admirable nobility.
your hurt and restored heart
still pretends to surprised find
all the things I have not said.

Your always empty messages
that arrive each morning,
my always present cup
that fills my soul with coffee.

And that sad look
without compassion shines
to make my journey look
like the mission is hard.
I see you and I fall,
I admire you but don't know
not a bit from your world
nor a lot from your word.

Let the time keep rolling
while it stays a seed
which can grow into something
that will be sublime.

Let the time fly next to me
and far away as well
let it not stop, keep fast
to wherever it wants to reach.

Little by little the changes
that exist and we don't observe,
will transform life into pages
we will be proud of conserve.

Enjoying each stage
every noise and silence,
I will nothing complain,
all of it will be rewarded.

SPECIALIST AMNESIA

It looks like I suffer some kind of amnesia.
Often I don't drink the coffee in the breakfast,
I forget the names of almost every street
but I can remember faces in great detail.

I have forgotten the name of many songs
but I know the phrases with such precision
that I carry in my mind a bunch of sentences
to use the one that better fits in any occasion.

You may believe this is how to create a story,
I like to think I have a specialist memory.
I don't select what to remember,
But I promise I always look back on November.

I don't think, by instance, in etiquette rules,
as I think of your smile or your restless eyes.
I can't recall all the mates from my school,
just the lessons from my teachers resound.

By choice I remember the smell of the soil
when is wet with water instead of with tears.
I'm not certain if what it was I forget
or when I decided to forward turn page.

But you can be sure I will never forget
every single moment with you I shared.
Even the dreams where you are, not knowing it,
occupy in my mind the space of a memory.

My amnesia is specialist in forgetting things
that don't make me big, that don't leave a mark.
For if our pass for this world is a shooting star,
would be a sin to keep a useless remind.

And if someone believes it's useless to remind
of me
erase it quickly, I don't want to use
the place from a memorial of a graceful dream
which perhaps might help to forgetness reduce.

I WILL HEAL

I don't know what I expect,
I don't know what I want,
I just know that inside,
little by little, I die.

What is that I desire?
How to know if I'm able
to get up and fly
into far away skies?

I think all day long,
I feel all day long,
but I lie a lot
when I'm feeling lost.

When what I look for
doesn't come soon
I rapidly judge
that I was a fool.

Silently I pray
as if it was a game,
appealing for a kiss
that can save me from this.

And when I supplicate,
I can feel the shine
of the riverdance,
coming from the gate.

Then I look at me.
I smile and move,
because this mess is
what I find so cool.

This is what I choose
where in times I drink
and gracefully I see
how all gets so blue

And I don't fall,
I just try to dance
and I only enjoy
and steal a glance.

Where do I come from?
Everything I know
is I need a word
to confess my love.

URGENT

Urgent is the superpower of distinguish evil
from good
and the pleasure to choose the second over the
first one.
Urgent is the magic of transform bitternes in
laugh
and to look for liberate all reprimed feelings
gone.

It is urgent to desire the simply, the human, the
austere,
emotional reconciliation, the sibling's peace.
A shower in town, a friendly handshake,
and like elderies, a soft and slow step.

To not pretend to be wise just for follow a guru,
sincere humbleness, disinterested friendship,
to plant a tree and care for it for many years,
watch the walk and don't let anything bother
you.

Say hi to the neighbor, visit grandmother,
dedicate a song, write a poem,
listen the parents, lull the children,
count the stars and feel the breathing.

Trust more and doubt less,
more understanding and less judgement,
more effort, less wishing,
less complains and more enjoyment.

More give and less demand,
more thanks and less ask,
to accept that we are hurt
and look for a cure.

ABOUT DREAMS AND REALITIES

Today I saw an orange sheep between the cotton clouds
that silently declined with the sun, and my heart rejoiced.
I sleep hugging the Moon and I tell her
all about the dreams I want to make come true.
Then my thoughts amaze me
when I wake up and they turn to you.

I have seen the wind telling the sea about two crazies he saw
so charmingly hugged when he caressed them,
and the jealous sea answered that some day
they will be happy sailing in his waters.
What they don't know, my life,
is that dreaming we have gone beyond that.

And the truth is I never even thought of you,
I never believed it existed someone like this,
who erases the sky with a kiss and paint it again with a smile.
And the truth is I don't want to lose you,
I never thought it existed a love like this,

with fairy taled knights and princesses with crimson lips.
And if this dream looks strange, you should know I learned from you,
that I am happy when you are next to me, and I don’t plan to let you go.

YOU DON'T GO (to my brother)

Not content being popular
you decided to give your life
to a woman who filled your soul
and you decided to love.

I confess you some jealous I had
when you said you wanted to live
all your lifetime with her, and I felt
like some part of me left.

If there is anithing hard to see
is we are not yesterdays' children.
years ago we don't go to feed
the ducks in Chapultepec lake.

But today I see you are happy
and I only can think
in all the things you build
and in my life they are still.

So you don't go
you just make bigger
the amount of plates
in our mom's dinner room.

And there will be more
kids running along
and gifts to be opened
when we spend Christmas along.

DON'T LET IT BE IN NOVEMBER

I want you to imagine I die.
Not being fatalist, we all are going to die.
But, if you knew this is the last February,
Which gesture would you say goodbye with?

If tomorrow and the next day
and the next year, I'm not longer in this world,
What difference would it make?
Would you cry the day whole?

That which you want to say before I go,
I'm still here to listen and respond.
Anything you may want to share.
don't let it be on an altar in November.

Tell me today, no matter if it is a claim..
Even if you had kept a secret for a long
I will understand if it comes with a hug
and the nude truth on the side.

Now go and do the same with all,
don't let pending words or kisses,
dances and flowers, laughs and moments

with people you live along.

So in the end, no sadness will be
no tears to permit,
only memories of the beauty
time that God let us have.

THIS IS LIFE ABOUT

Old dirty curtains try to cloud my sight,
not always making it, for the curiosity I was given
makes me find a hole where I can spy
and what I find I love, that I can't deny.

Brushstrokes create dark and shiny clouds in the sky,
all mixed over the horizon, contrasting with alive colors.
They are stunning, dazzling, and sometimes desperating
because I can't reach them with my muted clamors.

I've been told to resign, but why? I don't understand.
Is it family of giving up? Then I don't want to, I don't work like that.
I work fighting straight, even making others freaking out
because some are bothered being noticed when they try.

I don't know so many new and old things.

Suddenly my thoughts are alien to me,
they sail between the knowledge and the beauty
always choosing the road of persist.

Try, fail, give up and make.
Is the route for success.
The recipe for life.
Laugh, cry, learn and conquer.
Share and let the world go by.

DOPAMINE

I slept late
waiting for sleep to come
that in these new days
ran with no prior notice.

I wait for hours
and while waiting I look
for rise myself with the power
of a lambrusco and a book.

My mobile comes through
and dopamine grabs me
makes me docile
although I know it kills me.

By taking away my time
making me believe I live
while inside I feel
how I lost sighs.

How did I stop writing?
phrases of love and joy,
all that without elixir
I used to make fly and deploy.

In some corner of my mind
dormant memories live
waiting for you to wake them up
to start a new writing piece.

www.ingramcontent.com/pod-product-compliance
Lightning Source LLC
Chambersburg PA
CBHW051742130826
49812CB00033B/971
* 9 7 8 9 3 5 7 2 1 0 3 9 3 *